A PARENT'S WORKBOOK 2:

SEARCHING, DISCUSSING AND STUDYING SCRIPTURES

By

Teresa Billingsley

ISBN: 978-1-946662-02-6

Disclaimer

"*A Parent's Workbook 2: Searching, Discussing & Studying Scriptures*" was written to provide accurate and current information. Ideally it was written for parents and their teenagers to study The Bible while having important discussions about present-day issues. It is not intended to substitute for personal advice from a sound spiritual or parental leader. If you have any immediate questions or matters, and you need one-on-one counseling to address your specific situation, it is important that you seek the services of a qualified licensed professional in your area to address your particular concerns.

The opinions expressed in this book are those of the author's and should not be construed as representing the opinions of any particular religion or translation of The Bible. It is recommended that you read the relevant scriptures cited for clarification.

Dedication

I dedicate this book to my lord and savior, Jesus Christ, first and foremost. Second, in honor of introducing me to the scriptures and living a godly life in front of me, I pay homage to my mother (Bertha Billingsley) as well. Finally, to the parents, communities, relatives, youth groups, volunteers and ministries who strives to find ways to bridge the gap between parents and their teens, I wrote this book for you and with you in mind.

Acknowledgement

I am grateful for the word of God. It provides sustenance and guidance in every aspect of life. I strongly recommend The Bible as the primary source of sound counsel. If you are open and receptive to it, you will gain knowledge and wisdom for all that ails you.

I urge anyone interested in making your relationship with youth the best it could possibly be to research the scriptures. Also, humbly learn from both mature and baby Christians who search the word, speak the truth in love and who will cover you in prayer.

Introduction

To maximize the benefits and educational value of this study you should have gone through my online courses, "Anger Management" & "4 Personality Types." If you have not experienced these courses, then some of the questions you may be unable to answer and expound on. Some of the terms and personality types may be foreign to you. However, the scriptures are still relevant and captivating enough to have provided you with an array of topics to create some great discussions.

You are not constrained to my questions, they may assist you in coming up with your own that you find more relevant and specific to your family and problems you may currently be facing.

My primary goal is to do one thing. I want to inspire you to hunger for a relationship with God. I would like to wet the palate of youth to cause them to thirst after the word of God and want to search the scriptures. I personally do not have all the answers and I am constantly evolving and continue to be a work in progress.

Whether you are new to the scriptures or have studied them a long time and have the entire bible memorized, there is always much you can learn. You do not have to be intimidated or apprehensive about studying God's word. Think of it as a love letter or as a will. Enjoy all that He has to say to you and be encouraged!

Table of Contents

Disclaimer..IV
Dedication...VI
Acknowledgement...............................VIII
Introduction..X
Table of Contents.............................XIII
Instructions 1

Questions
Abigail & Nabal – 1 Samuel 25.........................6
Achan – Joshua 7......................................15
Jeroboam – 1 Kings 13................................25
Bartimaeus – Mark 10:46-52 & Luke 18:33-43......32
Born Blind – John 9....................................37

Answers
Abigail & Nabal – 1 Samuel 25.........................47
Achan – Joshua 7......................................63
Jeroboam – 1 Kings 13................................79
Bartimaeus – Mark 10:46-52 & Luke 18:33-43......90
Born Blind – John 9....................................96

Suggestions...109
Helpful Scriptures...................................113
Letter from the Author.............................117
Prayer of Salvation.................................120

Instructions

There are a variety of ways to use this workbook to your benefit. Parents are welcome to do the study themselves first and then go through it with your teenagers. Adults may elect to read the assigned passages together or separately and then discuss what was read with your teens.

You can decide to answer all the questions in writing and compare answers; the adults may want to break the questions up into different sessions; or pick and choose a set of questions you want your teens to answer.

Make any adjustments you want, the important thing is to dive in and let God lead you. The one thing I ask you to follow through with is the initial exercise. It is imperative that you read the scripture references assigned and write a summary of what you read. This is critical because it causes each participant to explain the just of what the verses meant to them. Having to condense it forces you to think in order to make your summary concise.

Having to individually complete this portion of the assignment helps you to get your own revelation and not be influenced by the opinions of others. What someone else chooses to write and share does not make what you wrote any less valuable or less profound.

In the section of this book with the answers, there may be a number preceding the answer. This number represents the verse in the chapter you were asked to read, that I base my response on. You may have a different answer based on the same verse or a different verse, and if so this is perfectly okay. This simply makes the discussions you will have more interesting and enjoyable.

Feel free to boldly express your point of view with humility and back it up with scripture references. Ultimately, have fun, be enlightened and enjoy what God has to say to you.

Questions

Abigail and Nabal

I.   The assigned reading for this bible study is <u>1 Samuel 25</u>

II.   Once you have finished reading the above listed passages of scripture answer the two below questions:

1.   Sum up this reading assignment in 50 words or less.

2.   What did you learn from reading these scriptures that relate to what you are currently dealing with?

- ______________________________________
- ______________________________________
- ______________________________________
- ______________________________________
- ______________________________________
- ______________________________________
- ______________________________________

- _________________________________
- _________________________________
- _________________________________
- _________________________________

III.   What new insight did you gain from discussing this with others? What did they help you see in the passage that you overlooked and can apply in your daily living? What unique perspective did someone else add that you found beneficial?

Abigail and Nabal

Read 1 Samuel 25 to assist you in answering the below questions.

Questions:

1. Who died in the beginning?
2. Who gathered together?
3. Where was the deceased buried?
4. Who rose up and where did he go?
5. Where was Nabal?
6. What was Nabal's economic status?
7. List the type of wealth he had?
8. What was he doing in Carmel?
9. What was the name of Nabal's wife?
10. How is his wife described?
11. Nabal was a descendant of what family?
12. How fair was Nabal in his business dealings?
13. What did David hear Nabal was doing?
14. How many did David send out?
15. What was David's instructions to those he sent?
16. Whose name were they to greet Nabal in?

17. They were to wish peace unto whom and/or what?
18. What was the message Nabal was to be reminded of?
19. What type of people was Nabal to confirm this information with?
20. What was Nabal asked to give?
21. Did David's men deliver the message as specified?
22. Was Nabal cooperative and receptive? Explain
23. Was Nabal the type of guy who shared if he didn't see any benefit in it for himself? Explain
24. What did David's men do next?
25. What did David do when he heard about Nabal's response?
26. How many men were used and what tasks were they given?
27. What did one messenger do that was significant?
28. How does the scripture describe the wise messenger who sought help to fix the problem Nabal caused?
29. Who did it appear this messenger sided with?
30. What did the messenger suggest?
31. Was Nabal a man that could be reasoned with? Explain
32. Did the messenger believe David would overlook Nabal's reply? Explain
33. Who did the messenger confide in hoping this person would resolve the situation?
34. What did this confidant gather together and take?
35. Did this person tell their spouse what they were doing? Explain
36. In this case, was it a good thing to keep this secret, or should there never be secrets? Explain
37. Was Abigail a timid woman, or did she behave courageous? Explain
38. Have you ever done anything similar to what Nabal did? Explain

39. Have you ever been ungrateful of someone who looked after you and blessed you, only to rudely turn them away when they asked something simple of you? Explain
40. Have you ever had someone like Nabal in your life who treated you badly when all you did was treat them well? Explain
41. What did David say that let us know what was fueling his anger?
42. In your own words, what was David's primary complaint?
43. Nabal broke one of David's personal rules. What distorted thinking is this an example of?
44. What rules do your parents have that are similar to David's rule?
45. Was it foolish of Nabal to be so dismissive of David's request? Explain
46. Have you ever behaved like Nabal to someone who had authority over you? Explain
47. List examples where David showed signs of unforgiveness:
48. What advice & scripture could you have given David, that if he followed, would have prevented him from getting upset?
49. Was Abigail initially smug when she approached David? Explain
50. Did she start out defending her husband and giving excuses? Explain
51. When she plead her case before David, who did she blame for not being hospitable to his young men?
52. Why did she say this person did not greet his young men proper?
53. What does the name Nabal mean?
54. Would she have had a different result had she been disrespectful to David and began telling David what to do and not do? Explain

55. Did she ask David to teach her husband a lesson, or demand that she be heard? Explain
56. Have your parents ever had to ask someone for mercy on you for something you did? Explain
57. What two things did she say were reasons why Nabal was inappropriate? Do you agree?
58. The messenger also agreed with one of these reasons, explain:
59. What is your name and what does it mean?
60. When others look at the way you carry yourself, do they associate you as a child under the authority of adults who are teaching you good things or bad things? Why?
61. Has anyone ever told you that your behavior is bad because of who your father or mother is? Explain
62. If you have absent parents or parents that are not teaching you the right things to do, is it still possible to learn the right morals and values and how to live on biblical principles? Explain
63. In verse 25 Abigail was asking David to overlook Nabal's behavior, what was her reasons why?
64. In verse 26 what was Abigail's logic for David not to pursue Nabal?
65. Have you ever been told to disregard what another person has said or done to you like Abigail asked David? Explain
66. What did Abigail do to pacify David's anger?
67. What convincing thought did she cause David to consider?
68. Was David angry with Abigail for wasting his time and delaying his battle? Explain
69. Who did David credit for Abigail's wise actions?
70. Did David consider Abigail's advice good or bad?
71. What did David acknowledge Abigail prevented him from doing?

72. What does this remind you and I to do when we are angry and ready to seek revenge?
73. Put any portion of what David said in verses 32 or 33 into your own words:
74. What did David admit would have happened by morning if Abigail had not intervened?
75. What reassurance did David give her?
76. When Abigail returned home what did she experience that further let her know that Nabal was a fool?
77. What personality type does Nabal appear to be? Explain the behavior Nabal displays that are shared with this personality type:
78. Did she immediately tell Nabal what she had done on his behalf?
79. Did she eventually tell Nabal? If yes, when?
80. What was Nabal's reaction?
81. Did Nabal suffer a curse as Abigail predicted? When and what if anything happened to Nabal?
82. When David heard of Nabal's fate, did he regret not carrying out his plan 11 days earlier? Explain
83. What two did David credit for the situation working out with Nabal without his intervention?
84. What message did David send to Abigail when he heard what happened to Nabal?
85. Where was Abigail when she received the message from David?
86. Did it appear this message was well received by Abigail or did it upset her? Explain
87. What was the next thing Abigail did in response to David's message?
88. List some of the things your parents do for you that you should thank them for:

89. When was the last time you acted like Nabal and feel
    ashamed for it?

Achan

I.   The assigned reading for this bible study is <u>Joshua 7</u>

II.   Once you have finished reading the above listed passages of scripture answer the two below questions:

1. Sum up this reading assignment in 50 words or less.

2. What did you learn from reading these scriptures that relate to what you are currently dealing with?

- ____
  ____
- ____
  ____
- ____
  ____
- ____
  ____
- ____
  ____
- ____
  ____

- _______________
- _______________
- _______________
- _______________

III.   What new insight did you gain from discussing this with others? What did they help you see in the passage that you overlooked and can apply in your daily living? What unique perspective did someone else add that you found beneficial?

Achan – Joshua 7

Read Joshua 7 to assist you in answering the below questions.

Questions

(1) Who is said to be angry in the beginning?
(2) What caused the anger to be kindled?
(3) What did Joshua do before landing an attack?
(4) Often before your enemies pick a fight with you they have studied you too and know your strengths and weaknesses. Those who know you, what would they say are your anger triggers?
(5) When Joshua's men followed his instructions, what did they report?
(6) Did their assessment prove to be true? What was the result?
(7) How far were they chased?
(8) Were there any casualties? If there were, how many were there?
(9) Whose hearts melted with fear?
(10) What did Joshua do (to his clothes) that was an example back then that a person was enraged?

(11) Have you ever released your anger like Joshua did? What have you done that is similar to this, where you have gotten angry and destroyed your own property?

(12) What else did Joshua and the elders of Israel do?

(13) Who did Joshua blame for this? Explain

(14) Have you ever blamed God, your parents or someone else when you have been deeply hurt by someone else or suffered loss? Explain

(15) Is it a good thing to project your anger onto people who did not do anything wrong to you? Explain

(16) What do you think Joshua meant when he said, would to God we had been content, and dwelt on the other side Jordan!"

(17) Have you ever asked God or your parents for something then when you got it regretted what it ended up costing you (ultimately, in the long run) or what you had to do, sacrifice, give up, or pay to get it? Explain

(18) Do you let fear of what could happen prevent you from trying to achieve? Explain

(19) How would you interpret this statement made by Joshua, "What can I say now that Israel had fled from its enemies?" Does it sound like he had given up?

(20) What was the concern the Israelites had regarding their reputation and the type of reaction it may generate?

(21) Have you ever worried about what others thought about your performance in a fight? Explain

(22) What distorted thinking is this an example of?

(23) What is your opinion of Joshua's statement, "They will come kill us and there will not be anyone to carry on your great name"?

(24) Have you heard friends or family make similar statements?

(25) What anger pattern has a person upset predicting that something bad is going to happen?

(26) When you speak negatively and lose hope what type of interpretation of your circumstances do you have, negative or positive?

(27) Are you likely to react calm or desperate?

(28) What are some counterpunches Joshua should have used?

(29) What simple command did God give Joshua that probably woke him and let him know he needed to do something and not wallow on the ground in self-pity?

(30) What did the Lord ask Joshua?

(31) When you have whined and thrown a tantrum has anyone ever calmly asked you, "What is your problem?" or "Why are you acting like that?" Explain

(32) Have you been told to stop crying, stop whining, stand up straight, dry your tears, shush, or be quiet and then you realized how you were behaving after it was pointed out? Did it wake you up and make you aware? Explain

(33) How did Israel sin?

(34) Did they suffer any consequences for their sin? If yes, explain

(35) When we sin does it cause a separation between us and God? Explain

(36) What has sin cost you?

(37) Have your sins ever caused a separation in your relationships? Explain

(38) Have you ever sinned against your parents, felt guilty and no longer able to face them, be around them comfortably or look them in the eyes? Explain

(39) What did the Lord tell the people to do the next day?

(40) What did the Lord say was necessary for them to fix their problem?

(41) What time of day did all the tribes come forward and present themselves?

(42) What was the plan to identify the one(s) guilty?

(43) What was to be the punishment of the guilty person(s)?

(44) Was this punishment too severe? Explain

(45) Should the guilty person(s) have had a trial? Explain

(46) If we handled these things this way today, do you think we would have the many prolonged problems we have?

(47) What time of day did Joshua comply?

(48) What tribe, family and individual was singled out and identified as the culprit?

(49) What did Joshua ask the one identified to do?

(50) What did he mean by this?

(51) What did Joshua tell the one identified not to do?

(52) What did Achan admit to?

(53) Should he have admitted all he did? Why not find out what Joshua knew first?

(54) Why not assert his right to be silent?

(55) What rights did Achan have that he surrendered?

(56) Should he have gotten legal counsel first?

(57) Should Achan have been afforded time to think before responding?

(58) How is this old method different than today?

(59) Should we go back to the old method? Explain

(60) In your opinion, is the new method better? Why or why not?

(61) List the differences and pros and cons of justice then and now.

(62) Which of the five senses caused Achan's initial temptation?

(63) What commandment(s) did he admit to breaking immediately thereafter?

(64) Describe what was among the spoil.

(65) Where did Joshua's messengers recover the stolen property?

(66) How did they know where to find it?

(67) Why did they not punish Achan immediately after he confessed?

(68) Why do you think they ran to confirm and retrieve the items first?

(69) They brought the items from Achan's tent to Joshua, and all the children of Israel and laid them before the Lord. Do you think they withheld any of the loot for themselves? Why?

(70) If you were a messenger would you bring it all back or keep some? Why?

(71) Why was it important to occur in front of all the children of Israel?

(72) What did Joshua and all Israel take and bring to the valley of Achor?

(73) Is there a reason why Achan and everything that belonged to him or was associated with him was collected together?

(74) Why not preserve some of the things of value and use them? Explain

(75) As Joshua said, "Why did you bring this trouble on us? Now the Lord shall trouble you." What did they do to punish Achan and discourage this from happening again?

(76) Was the punishment more impactful by everyone participating and it being a public display?

(77) Did you know the family could also receive punishment for something one of their relatives did?

(78) Do you know of other examples in The Bible of this process?

(79) If this happened today, would you like to be responsible if your parents or siblings sinned?

(80) Your parents are responsible for violations you commit against others, is this fair? Explain

(81) Why should you listen to your parents when they instruct you to do things that the Lord God agrees you are to obey, and you locate scriptures that also agree?

(82) Do you see ways that diverting from seeking the Lord has made crime, sin, corruption, and rebellion worse? Explain

(83) Long ago the people decided they no longer wanted God to be the only judge (1 Samuel 8), and demanded to have a king rule them. Has this decision helped or hurt us?

(84) What was piled on Achan?

(85) What was the place named where this happened at?

(86) Why do you think God was so angry?

(87) Was God's anger needless?

(88) Was God's anger just?

(89) Was God's anger causing a problem?

(90) Would a leader in the armed services be just as angry, if a soldier chose not to follow orders, and committed an isolated act against direct orders to profit, and it cost other soldiers' lives?

(91) Do you think soldiers are aware of all the reasons they are ordered to act and fight?

(92) Is it a soldier's job to know all the reasons or to just follow orders?

(93) As youth with your parents being responsible and forced to answer for your actions should you be entitled to know all the facts, rationale and reasons before you obey, or should you just obey? Explain

(94) Are the things your parents tell you to do for your own good and to teach you responsibility? Explain

(95) Should you ever question your parents' orders when they are in compliance with God's laws and the moral code adopted by society.

(96) If the orders agree with man's laws but disagrees with God's laws, which should prevail?

NOTES

Jeroboam

I.   The assigned reading for this bible study is <u>1 Kings 13</u>

II.   Once you have finished reading the above listed passages of scripture answer the two below questions:

1. Sum up this reading assignment in 50 words or less.

2. What did you learn from reading these scriptures that relate to what you are currently dealing with?

- ____
- ____
- ____
- ____
- ____
- ____

* ______________________________
* ______________________________
* ______________________________
* ______________________________

III.   What new insight did you gain from discussing this with others? What did they help you see in the passage that you overlooked and can apply in your daily living? What unique perspective did someone else add that you found beneficial?

Jeroboam – 1 Kings 13

Please read 1 Kings 13 for the answers to the questions below.

Questions

1. The first individual mentioned in this chapter was characterized by what three words?
2. Where was he said to come out of?
3. How?
4. Where was he going?
5. Where was Jeroboam and what was he doing?
6. A child was said to born unto whose house?
7. What was the child supposed to be named?
8. What was said to be burnt upon him?
9. What was given to say the Lord had spoken?
10. When was it given?
11. What proof would evidence the Lord had spoken?
12. Who heard the saying of the messenger?
13. Who was the messenger who delivered the saying?
14. What did he put forth from the altar?
15. What did he say?
16. How does the NLT version of scripture describe Jeroboam's mood and actions?

17. What symptoms did Jeroboam exhibit of his mood?
18. What happened next?
19. Did his prophesy come true?
20. Explain how the prophesy did or did not come true:
21. Who asked the man of God to entreat the Lord?
22. What did he want the man of God to ask for or do?
23. Did the man of God comply?
24. Explain how the man of God did or did not comply:
25. What did the king say to the man of God?
26. Did the man of God accept?
27. What did the man of God reply?
28. What did the man of God say that inspired and charged his response?
29. What directive did he say he was given?
30. Who did he say gave him this charge?
31. Did he obey?
32. How did he obey or disobey?
33. Word spread to who by his relatives of what happened?
34. Where was this person when his relatives told him?
35. What did his relatives tell him?
36. How were these relatives related to him?
37. Where did the relatives see the man of God coming from?
38. What did the man ask his relatives?
39. What did the prophet direct his relatives to do next?
40. Did his relatives obey? Explain
41. What did the prophet do with the donkey?
42. What did he chase after?
43. Did he find who or what he was looking for? Explain
44. What did he ask?
45. What reply did he receive?
46. What invitation did he give?
47. What response did his invitation receive?

48. What rationalize was given to accept or reject the invitation?
49. Did he owe an explanation as to why he refused the invitation? Explain
50. Does who is making the inquiry matter as to whether or not you should answer? Explain
51. Should we simply obey what God and our parents tell us without qualifying our actions? Explain
52. Who, in history, was an early example of saying too much when encouraged to defy God's rules?
53. What other times have you told others "no" and felt the need to explain why? Give examples
54. What advice would you give someone who is uncertain whether to abide by their parent's rules?
55. What excuses have you heard people give as to why they defied a trusted authority's rules?
56. What connection was pointed out to try to garner the invited person's trust?
57. Who did the prophet say spoke to him?
58. By whose authority?
59. What did the prophet claim he was told to tell the man of God?
60. Had the prophet told the truth?
61. Was the man of God swayed by the prophet? Explain
62. Who did the word of the Lord come upon at the prophet's home?
63. Where were they when this happened?
64. Did the man of God deserve chastisement? Explain
65. Who did God have admonish the man of God?
66. What was the man of God told were his initial mistakes?
67. What else was the man of God told he did wrong?
68. What was he denied?

69. What did the prophet do after the man of God finished eating?
70. What misfortune did the man of God encounter once he left?
71. Who or what stood by the man of God's carcass?
72. Did the old prophet ever find out what happened to the man of God? Explain
73. When the old prophet heard the news he knew it was the man of God this had happened to. How could he be so confident?
74. Who did the old prophet say delivered the man of God and to whom?
75. According to the old prophet was the man of God's death random and unpredictable? Explain
76. What did the old prophet direct to be done next?
77. Did the prophet find what he went looking for? Explain
78. What else did he notice with the carcass that was unusual?
79. What did the old prophet do next?
80. Where was the carcass buried?
81. How did the old prophet react upon laying the man of God's carcass in his own grave?
82. What term of endearment did he use for the man of God?
83. Would you have responded like the old prophet? Explain
84. What did the old prophet tell his sons to do with his body when he died?
85. Why did he say he was making this request?
86. Did Jeroboam change his life and repent? Explain
87. What was the end result of Jeroboam?

❖ Read Proverbs 6 and list the scriptures that would have been good for Jeroboam to have been mindful of:

NOTES

Bartimaeus

I.   The assigned reading for this bible study is <u>Mark 10:46-52 & Luke 18:35-43</u>

II.   Once you have finished reading the above listed passages of scripture answer the two below questions:

1. Sum up this reading assignment in 50 words or less.

2. What did you learn from reading these scriptures that relate to what you are currently dealing with?

- ____
- ____
- ____
- ____
- ____
- ____

- ____
  ____
- ____
  ____
- ____
  ____
- ____
  ____

III.   What new insight did you gain from discussing this with others? What did they help you see in the passage that you overlooked and can apply in your daily living? What unique perspective did someone else add that you found beneficial?

Bartimaeus – Mark 10:46-52 & Luke 18:35-43

Read Mark 10:46-52 & Luke 18:35-43 to assist you in answering the below questions.

Questions

1. What revered person came to Jericho?
2. What others were said to be with this person?
3. Whose son sat by the highway?
4. What was his name?
5. What was he doing there?
6. He was he characterized as having what disability?
7. What got his attention? What did he see?
8. What did he ask people?
9. What was he told?
10. Did he know this passerby personally?
11. Why do you believe he called out to this passerby?
12. What did he call out to him saying?
13. Who reacted and what was the reaction?
14. Why do you think others reacted to him this way?
15. Did others' reaction and criticism affect him?
16. Why do you think he was able to dismiss them?

17. Have you let the comments and critiques of others cause you to lose out on a blessing from God? Explain
18. What did the passerby do as a result?
19. What hypocritical thing did the critics do when the passerby was receptive to him?
20. What should this tell you about people?
21. What did the passerby ask him?
22. State his answer to the question:
23. How did Jesus respond?
24. What did Jesus tell him to do?
25. What did Jesus say made him whole and saved this man?
26. How long did it take before the man saw any results? What were the results if any?
27. Who got credit in the end? Explain
28. How did the two books of The Bible differ in how they ended this story?

NOTES

Born Blind

I.   The assigned reading for this bible study is <u>John 9</u>

II.   Once you have finished reading the above listed passages of scripture answer the two below questions:

1. Sum up this reading assignment in 50 words or less.

2. What did you learn from reading these scriptures that relate to what you are currently dealing with?

- ____
- ____
- ____
- ____
- ____
- ____
- ____
- ____

- _______________________________________
- _______________________________________
- _______________________________________

III. What new insight did you gain from discussing this with others? What did they help you see in the passage that you overlooked and can apply in your daily living? What unique perspective did someone else add that you found beneficial?

Born Blind – John 9

Read John 9 to assist you in answering the below questions.

Questions

1. Jesus was passing by and noticed a man with what type of condition?
2. How long had he been in that condition?
3. What did Jesus' disciples attribute to the cause of this man's condition?
4. What question did his disciples ask him regarding who was responsible for the man's condition?
5. How did Jesus respond?
6. Interpret what you believe Jesus meant by this response:
7. What did Jesus make and how did he make it?
8. What did he do next?
9. If you heard this going on by you would you have remained and let this happen to you if you were this man? Explain
10. Jesus instructed this man to do what?
11. What word is interpreted and what is the interpretation?
12. Did the man do what Jesus instructed him to?
13. What resulted?

14. People who knew him when they saw him, what did they wonder about?
15. Who were these people?
16. What were people heard saying?
17. Did the man have anything to say? Explain
18. The people wanted to know what about this man?
19. How did he answer?
20. Then what did they want to know?
21. What did the man answer?
22. What did the people do next?
23. Was there any significance to when Jesus healed this man?
24. Why was this a problem?
25. What did the Pharisees want to know of this man?
26. What did the man answer?
27. What did the Pharisees surmise from the information the man gave them?
28. Why did they draw this conclusion?
29. What did others think of Jesus?
30. Were the Pharisees and others' opinions aligned about Jesus? Explain
31. Today, does everyone agree about who Jesus is? Explain
32. They asked the man who was healed his opinion of what Jesus did to him, what did he say?
33. Was the man who was healed asked this only once?
34. Explain why you think that was?
35. Is there a danger in trying to prove how the Lord works? Should it matter?
36. What is your best evidence of the Lord working in your life?
37. What was the next attempt that was made to derail the healing?
38. Who did the Jews summon that changed their opinion?
39. What 3 questions did they ask these experts?

40. How did they answer the 3 questions?
41. What other question were they also obviously asked based on their added reply? List the possible question along with their answer:
42. What did they say to remove the spotlight from on them?
43. Who and what were these experts afraid of?
44. Do you think their involvement with the synagogue was important to them? Explain
45. Who did they call next to question?
46. What did they say to this person?
47. Was there anything wrong with what they said to this person?
48. Did this person argue with the advice he was given? Explain
49. What fact did he point out that the Jews could not refute?
50. What did they question him about next?
51. Would these questions have gotten you angry? Explain
52. How did the man respond?
53. Did this man feel heard? Explain
54. What question(s) did the man ask them as a reply?
55. How did the Jews respond to him?
56. What anger patterns and styles did the Jews demonstrate?
57. Did the Jews give a mature or immature reply? Explain
58. Who did they compare Jesus to?
59. Did Jesus measure up to this other person in their opinion? Explain
60. In your own words, what did the man have to say about what happened to him and how they were responding to it?
61. This man was not an expert in religious doctrine yet what did he say that demonstrated wisdom?
62. Did it appear the Jews were receptive to the man's logic and wisdom? Explain
63. What vanity was in full operation in the Jews and the

Pharisees?

64. Who was told the man had been cast out and searched for him until he found him?
65. What did Jesus ask him?
66. Was the man angry about being asked this question? Explain
67. If the Jews had asked this man the exact same question do you think he would have responded the same way?
68. Explain what may have been different to solicit a different reaction.
69. What did the man's response to Jesus show about his stance?
70. How did Jesus answer?
71. How much convincing did it take for the man to believe? Explain
72. What was Jesus' reply?
73. What do you think this statement means?
74. Did the Pharisees appear to understand what Jesus meant by his statement? Explain
75. What did Jesus say in response?

NOTES

Answers

Abigail and Nabal – 1 Samuel 25

Questions & Answers:

1. Who died in the beginning?
   - (1) Samuel died
2. Who gathered together?
   - (1) the Israelites
3. Where was the deceased buried?
   - (1) In his house at Ramah
4. Who rose up and where did he go?
   - (1) David arose, and went down to the wilderness of Paran
5. Where was Nabal?
   - (2) In Maon
6. What was Nabal's economic status?
   - (2) Very great
   - (6) prosperity (wealthy)
7. List the type of wealth he had?
   - (2) 3,000 sheep and 1,000 goats
8. What was he doing in Carmel?
   - (2) Shearing his sheep in Carmel
9. What was the name of Nabal's wife?

- (3) Abigail
10. How is his wife described?
    - (3) a woman of good understanding, of a beautiful countenance
11. Nabal was a descendant of what family?
    - (3) The house of Caleb
12. How fair was Nabal in his business dealings?
    - (3) churlish, evil, dishonest
13. What did David hear Nabal was doing?
    - (4) Shearing his sheep
14. How many did David send out?
    - (5) 10 young men
15. What was David's instructions to those he sent?
    - (5) get up to Carmel, go to Nabal
16. Whose name were they to greet Nabal in?
    - (5) David's name
17. They were to wish peace unto whom and/or what?
    - (6) Peace to thee (Nabal), peace to thine house, and peace to all he had
18. What was the message Nabal was to be reminded of?
    - (7) How David and his men protected Nabal's shepherds near Carmel, and all Nabal owned
19. What type of people was Nabal to confirm this information with?
    - (8) Their young men
20. What was Nabal asked to give?
    - (8) Whatever they had on hand
21. Did David's men deliver the message as specified?
    - (9) Yes
22. Was Nabal cooperative and receptive? Explain
    - (10) No

- (10) He commented, who does David think he is? He could be a fugitive on the run for all I know.
23. Was Nabal the type of guy who shared if he didn't see any benefit in it for himself? Explain
    - (11) No
    - (11) He said, why should he take his resources and give them to strangers? It's like saying, "Why should I be nice to them? What's in it for me?"
24. What did David's men do next?
    - (12) They returned to David and shared what Nabal had said to them
25. What did David do when he heard about Nabal's response?
    - (13) He told his men to prepare for battle
26. How many men were used and what tasks were they given?
    - (13) 400 men girded their sword, and two hundred stayed behind to guard property
27. What did one messenger do that was significant?
    - (14) He told Nabal's wife Abigail that David sent messengers to Nabal but Nabal disrespected the messengers and angered David
28. How does the scripture describe the wise messenger who sought help to fix the problem Nabal caused?
    - (14) one of the young men
29. Who did it appear this messenger sided with?
    - (15) David and his men who had been nice to them
    - (16) He acknowledged David's men protected them and their sheep day and night
30. What did the messenger suggest?
    - (17) That Abigail do something before evil came to them
31. Was Nabal a man that could be reasoned with? Explain
    - (17) No

- (17) The messenger described Nabal as a son of Belial/ill-tempered, who no one could talk to
32. Did the messenger believe David would overlook Nabal's reply? Explain
    - (17) No
    - (17) He knew there would be trouble and retaliation
33. Who did the messenger confide in hoping this person would resolve the situation?
    - (14) Abigail
34. What did this confidant gather together and take?
    - (18) 200 loaves, 2 bottles of wine, and five sheep ready dressed, 5 measures of parched corn, 100 clusters of raisins, and 200 cakes of figs
35. Did this person tell their spouse what they were doing? Explain
    - (19) No.
    - (19) She told not her husband Nabal
36. In this case, was it a good thing to keep this secret, or should there never be secrets? Explain
    - Optional – their honest answer to this question lends its way for great discussions
    - It was wise of Abigail not to tell Nabal, if he knew he would have potentially made matters worse
37. Was Abigail a timid woman, or did she behave courageous? Explain
    - (20) She was courageous
    - (20) She saw David and his men coming toward her and she did not lose her nerve and continued and met them, fully aware they were in war mode.
38. Have you ever done anything similar to what Nabal did? Explain

- Optional – their honest answer to this question lends its way for great discussions

39. Have you ever been ungrateful of someone who looked after you and blessed you, only to rudely turn them away when they asked something simple of you? Explain

- Optional – their honest answer to this question lends its way for great discussions
- Yes.
- I have had a bad attitude when my parents asked me to do chores – clean my room, wash dishes, mow the lawn, run an errand, babysit, etc.
- I made a bad comment to a teacher in class who asked me to read or turn in my homework
- My boss reprimanded me for being late and asked me to show up on time or I could lose my job. I quit and spread rumors about what a mean boss she or he is
- When my parents want me to get dressed for church, I purposely take my time, complain and try to make it difficult for them so they will get frustrated and let me stay home
- My parents will let me use the car and I will not put gas in it or treat them or the car respectfully. I drive reckless and throw a tantrum if they say no, until I get a yes
- When my mother comes to pick me up from school, I make her wait if I am talking to a friend or flirting with someone cute. I know she will not leave me and her threats are just bluffs, so I take my time sometimes to aggravate her on purpose.

40. Have you ever had someone like Nabal in your life who treated you badly when all you did was treat them well? Explain

- Optional – their honest answer to this question lends its way for great discussions
- A pet that you fed, clean up after, trained, saved allowance to buy and it bit you

41. What did David say that let us know what was fueling his anger?
    - (21) "Surely in vain have I kept all that this fellow hath in the wilderness, so that nothing was missed of all that pertained unto him: and he hath requited me evil for good."

42. In your own words, what was David's primary complaint?
    - (22) That he went out of his way to be good to Nabal and in return Nabal disrespected him and acted ungrateful

43. Nabal broke one of David's personal rules. What distorted thinking is this an example of?
    - Imperative Thinking

44. What rules do your parents have that are similar to David's rule?
    - A child should always be respectful to adults and those in authority over them
    - Parents feed, protect, love and give to their children, the least a child can do is to perform any reasonable task asked of them with a good attitude
    - When a child (under their authority) acts like they have forgotten the power a parent has, parents will be prone to issue judgement and punishment to give the child a reminder
    - When someone treats you kind, be appreciative. Do not be ungrateful, rude or act entitled

45. Was it foolish of Nabal to be so dismissive of David's request? Explain

- Optional – their honest answer to this question lends its way for great discussions
- Yes
- It was asking for trouble for Nabal to disregard and not reverence the position of those in authority over him

46. Have you ever behaved like Nabal to someone who had authority over you? Explain
   - Optional – their honest answer to this question lends its way for great discussions

47. List examples where David showed signs of unforgiveness:
   - He was keeping score
   - He felt entitled to some type of retribution or reward for doing the right thing
   - He felt owed for something that he had done for Nabal in the past
   - David expected Nabal to agree and felt Nabal had no right to say, "No"

48. What advice & scripture could you have given David, that if he followed, would have prevented him from getting upset?
   - Optional – their honest answer to this question lends its way for great discussions
   - Owe no man anything but love (Romans 13:8-10)
   - Love, give, or bless others and do it with a pure heart not expecting anything in return (Luke 6:35)
   - Let God see what you do in secret and He will reward you openly (Matthew 6:4)

49. Was Abigail initially smug when she approached David? Explain
   - (23) No
   - (23) She was humble. She fell before David on her face, and bowed herself to the ground

50. Did she start out defending her husband and giving excuses? Explain
    - (24) No.
    - (24) She fell at David's feet and took full responsibility and asked to take the punishment herself for what Nabal did.
51. When she plead her case before David, who did she blame for not being hospitable to his young men?
    - Optional – their honest answer to this question lends its way for great discussions
    - Herself
    - Nabal
52. Why did she say this person did not greet his young men proper?
    - (25) I did not know your men had come and I did not see them
    - (25) Please overlook Nabal's behavior, his name alone is telling that he is a man of Belial
53. What does the name Nabal mean?
    - Folly is with him
54. Would she have had a different result had she been disrespectful to David and began telling David what to do and not do? Explain
    - Optional – their honest answer to this question lends its way for great discussions
    - Yes
    - David had power and authority over them and could penalize them
    - David was already angry, it would not have gone well for her to upset him further
55. Did she ask David to teach her husband a lesson, or demand that she be heard? Explain

- (24) No, no
- (24) She begged David for mercy and asked for permission to speak to him

56. Have your parents ever had to ask someone for mercy on you for something you did? Explain
    - Optional – their honest answer to this question lends its way for great discussions
    - Yes
    - With my school, the court, a teacher, the police, a judge, my principal, my coach, etc.

57. What two things did she say were reasons why Nabal was inappropriate? Do you agree?
    - (25) He is a man of Belial
    - (25) He was destined to be a fool that is why he was named Nabal
    - I do not agree that his name made him destined a fool
    - Optional – their honest answer to this question lends its way for great discussions

58. The messenger also agreed with one of these reasons, explain:
    - (17) he said their master (Nabal) is such a son of Belial

59. What is your name and what does it mean?
    - Optional – their honest answer to this question lends its way for great discussions

60. When others look at the way you carry yourself, do they associate you as a child under the authority of adults who are teaching you good things or bad things? Why?
    - Optional – their honest answer to this question lends its way for great discussions

61. Has anyone ever told you that your behavior is bad because of who your father or mother is? Explain

- Optional – their honest answer to this question lends its way for great discussions
62. If you have absent parents or parents that are not teaching you the right things to do, is it still possible to learn the right morals and values and how to live on biblical principles? Explain
    - Optional – their honest answer to this question lends its way for great discussions
    - Yes
    - You can be connected to a positive mentor, attend a good church or youth program, and study the Bible and learn biblical principles yourself
63. In verse 25 Abigail was asking David to overlook Nabal's behavior, what was her reasons why?
    - Optional – their honest answer to this question lends its way for great discussions
    - (25) Nabal was not worth the trouble
    - (25) Nabal is a wicked and ill-tempered man. He is a fool, just ignore him
64. In verse 26 what was Abigail's logic for David not to pursue Nabal?
    - (26) Because God had allowed her to reach David before he carried out his revenge
    - (26) Let God seek out Nabal and get revenge and curse Nabal
65. Have you ever been told to disregard what another person has said or done to you like Abigail asked David? Explain
    - Optional – their honest answer to this question lends its way for great discussions
    - Boys are not to fight with girls, it's an uneven match
    - Don't beat up your younger or smaller siblings

- Do not talk back to your parents or another authority figure
66. What did Abigail do to pacify David's anger?
    - (27) She gave him the gifts she brought for David and his men (fed them food)
    - (28) She asked for his forgiveness
    - She acknowledged the wrong that was done to him
    - (28) She flattered him.
    - (28-29) She basically told David, Nabal would get what he deserved from God, why should David bother with him. David had so much going for him, the Lord would reward David with a lasting dynasty because the battles he fights are for the Lord, and evil is not found in David. Even when others seek to kill David, God protects David and keeps him safe. His enemies are not so fortunate, and can be brought down by the mere stone released from David's sling.
67. What convincing thought did she cause David to consider?
    - (30-31) When God makes you ruler over Israel, you do not want to look back on your life and have this one huge blemish on your record and in your conscience. You do not want to have the burden of how a foolish man, easily conquered by you, not worth your time and battle, you mercilessly killed who was no match for you and your ability.
68. Was David angry with Abigail for wasting his time and delaying his battle? Explain
    - (32) No
    - (32) He was grateful she stopped him and convinced him not to carry out his plans
69. Who did David credit for Abigail's wise actions?
    - (32) the Lord God of Israel

- (32) He said, "Praise the Lord, the God of Israel, who has sent you to me today!"

70. Did David consider Abigail's advice good or bad?
    - (33) good and blessed

71. What did David acknowledge Abigail prevented him from doing?
    - (33) thou has kept me this day from coming to shed blood, and from avenging myself with mine own hand

72. What does this remind you and I to do when we are angry and ready to seek revenge?
    - Don't take the law into your own hands
    - Let the person's parents/authority punish them, not you
    - Turn the situation over to God and let him take care of it
    - Don't be quick to retaliate when you are mad and feel offended

73. Put any portion of what David said in verses 32 or 33 into your own words:
    - Optional – their honest answer to this question lends its way for great discussions
    - Thank God He sent you to me
    - Thank you for talking sense into me
    - It is good you stopped me, I was about to do something stupid
    - I almost let my anger cause me to take a man's life
    - I was so mad I was about to kill a man with my bare hands

74. What did David admit would have happened by morning if Abigail had not intervened?
    - (34) he would have killed every man there with Nabal

75. What reassurance did David give her?

- (35) He told her she could return home in peace. He accepted her peace offerings (food) and would take her advice and not go after Nabal and not seek revenge

76. When Abigail returned home what did she experience that further let her know that Nabal was a fool?
    - (36) Nabal was throwing a party
    - (36) Nabal was drunk
    - (36) He was unprepared to defend himself had David showed up to attack him
    - (36) He was oblivious and completely ignorant of the danger his actions had put he and all the other men in

77. What personality type does Nabal appear to be? Explain the behavior Nabal displays that are shared with this personality type:
    - Optional – their honest answer to this question lends its way for great discussions
    - Funnies
    - He says and does things on impulse – turning David's men away
    - Funnies generally do not think, they just do/act
    - They do and say things without thinking
    - Like to party and have fun
    - Do not get it when they fail. A young man, and Abigail realized the foolish danger Nabal's action put him in, but Nabal had no clue and was known not to listen or understand the gravity of it all
    - Want fun right now, do not want to wait – Nabal got drunk

78. Did she immediately tell Nabal what she had done on his behalf?
    - (36) No

79. Did she eventually tell Nabal? If yes, when?
    - (36-37) Yes
    - (36-37) the following morning
80. What was Nabal's reaction?
    - (37) his heart died within him, and he became as a stone
81. Did Nabal suffer a curse as Abigail predicted? When and what if anything happened to Nabal?
    - Optional – their honest answer to this question lends its way for great discussions
    - (38) Yes
    - (38) Ten days later, the Lord struck Nabal and Nabal died
82. When David heard of Nabal's fate, did he regret not carrying out his plan 11 days earlier? Explain
    - (39) No
    - (39) He thanked the Lord for handling Nabal and was glad he had not sought his own revenge.
83. What two did David credit for the situation working out with Nabal without his intervention?
    - The Lord and Abigail
84. What message did David send to Abigail when he heard what happened to Nabal?
    - (39-40) He sent a proposal to Abigail and asked her to be his wife
85. Where was Abigail when she received the message from David?
    - (40) Carmel
86. Did it appear this message was well received by Abigail or did it upset her? Explain
    - (41) It was well received and humbled her. She got up and bowed to the earth. She even offered and was

willing to wash the feet of David's servants sent to deliver the proposal she was so excited

87. What was the next thing Abigail did in response to David's message?
    - (42) she quickly took five of her female servants with her, followed the messengers to David and became David's wife

88. List some of the things your parents do for you that you should thank them for:
    - Optional – their honest answer to this question lends its way for great discussions

89. When was the last time you acted like Nabal and feel ashamed for it?
    - Optional – their honest answer to this question lends its way for great discussions

Teresa Billingsley

NOTES

Achan – Joshua 7

Questions & Answers:

(1) Who is said to be angry in the beginning?
- (1) the Lord
(2) What caused the anger to be kindled?
- (1) The children of Israel committed a trespass and took of the accursed thing
(3) What did Joshua do before landing an attack?
- (2) he sent men from Jericho to Ai to spy out the city
(4) Often before your enemies pick a fight with you they have studied you too and know your strengths and weaknesses. Those who know you, what would they say are your anger triggers?
- Optional and variety of answers acceptable as long as they are honest
(5) When Joshua's men followed his instructions, what did they report?
- (4) Ai had so few people only 2,000-3,000 men would be enough to take them over
- (4) It wasn't necessary for all of them to go
(6) Did their assessment prove to be true? What was the result?
- (4) No.

- (4) About 3,000 men went and came back running in retreat

(7) How far were they chased?

- (5) The men of Ai chased the Israelites from before their city gate unto Shebarim

(8) Were there any casualties? If there were, how many were there?

- (5) Yes

- (5) 36

(9) Whose hearts melted with fear?

- (5) The Israelites

(10) What did Joshua do (to his clothes) that was an example back then that a person was enraged?

- (6) Joshua rent his clothes

(11) Have you ever released your anger like Joshua did? What have you done that is similar to this, where you have gotten angry and destroyed your own property?

- Optional – their honest answer to this question lends its way for great discussions

(12) What else did Joshua and the elders of Israel do?

- (6) they fell to the earth on their faces, before the ark of the Lord until the eventide (evening) and put dust upon their heads

(13) Who did Joshua blame for this? Explain

- (7) God

- (7) Joshua called out to God and asked (blamed God saying) "Why did you bring us across the Jordan River to deliver us into the hands of the Ammonites to destroy us?"

(14) Have you ever blamed God, your parents or someone else when you have been deeply hurt by someone else or suffered loss? Explain

- Optional – their honest answer to this question lends its way for great discussions

(15) Is it a good thing to project your anger onto people who did not do anything wrong to you? Explain

- No. It is a bad thing to release your anger onto an innocent person who has nothing to do with why you are angry

(16) What do you think Joshua meant when he said, "Would to God we had been content, and dwelt on the other side Jordan!"

- that he wished they had been satisfied with their prior situation and stayed where they were, then they would not have endured their recent tragedies

(17) Have you ever asked God or your parents for something then when you got it regretted what it ended up costing you (ultimately, in the long run) or what you had to do, sacrifice, give up, or pay to get it? Explain

- Optional – their honest answer to this question lends its way for great discussions

(18) Do you let fear of what could happen prevent you from trying to achieve? Explain

- Optional – their honest answer to this question lends its way for great discussions

(19) How would you interpret this statement made by Joshua, "What can I say now that Israel had fled from its enemies?" Does it sound like he had given up?

- Optional – their honest answer to this question lends its way for great discussions
- There is nothing left to say
- It's too late to try to fix this
- I am doomed because the damage has been done?
- Our reputation is that of losers. We have lost the battle and are seen as cowards. We cannot recover from this now, we give up
- Once you retreat there is nothing left to do

(20) What was the concern the Israelites had regarding their reputation and the type of reaction it may generate?

- When the Canaanites and all others find out/hear about it, they will surround us and wipe us off the face of the earth?

(21) Have you ever worried about what others thought about your performance in a fight? Explain

- Optional – their honest answer to this question lends its way for great discussions

- When word got out we ran or did not stand and fight, everyone else will pick fights with us or come kill us

(22) What distorted thinking is this an example of?

- Mind reading

(23) What is your opinion of Joshua's statement, "They will come kill us and there will not be anyone to carry on your great name"?

- It is an overly dramatic assessment

(24) Have you heard friends or family make similar statements?

- Optional – their honest answer to this question lends its way for great discussions

- Yes. If I do not show up to fight, then everybody will start challenging me and say I am weak

(25) What anger pattern has a person upset predicting that something bad is going to happen?

- anticipatory anger

(26) When you speak negatively and lose hope what type of interpretation of your circumstances do you have, negative or positive?

- negative

(27) Are you likely to react calm or desperate?

- desperate

(28) What are some counterpunches Joshua should have used?

- Optional – their honest answer to this question lends its way for great discussions
- "I will not lose hope!"
- "I have faith that God is with us and will bring us through this"

(29) What simple command did God give Joshua that probably woke him and let him know he needed to do something and not wallow on the ground in self-pity?

- (13) "Up (Get up)"

(30) What did the Lord ask Joshua?

- (13) "Why are you on your face?"

(31) When you have whined and thrown a tantrum has anyone ever calmly asked you, "What is your problem?" or "Why are you acting like that?" Explain

- Optional – their honest answer to this question lends its way for great discussions

(32) Have you been told to stop crying, stop whining, stand up straight, dry your tears, shush, or be quiet and then you realized how you were behaving after it was pointed out? Did it wake you up and make you aware? Explain

- Optional – their honest answer to this question lends its way for great discussions

(33) How did Israel sin?

- They went against God's covenant (written laws) and broke the laws He commanded them.
- They stole and took of the accursed thing and mingled it with their things

(34) Did they suffer any consequences for their sin? If yes, explain

- (12) they couldn't stand up to their enemies
- (12) retreated because they were cursed

- (12) God would no longer be with them until they destroyed the cursed things among them.

(35) When we sin does it cause a separation between us and God? Explain

- Optional – their honest answer to this question lends its way for great discussions
- Yes. Sin separates us from God (Isaiah 59:2)

(36) What has sin cost you?

- Optional – their honest answer to this question lends its way for great discussions

(37) Have your sins ever caused a separation in your relationships? Explain

- Optional – their honest answer to this question lends its way for great discussions

(38) Have you ever sinned against your parents, felt guilty and no longer able to face them, be around them comfortably or look them in the eyes? Explain

- Optional – their honest answer to this question lends its way for great discussions

(39) What did the Lord tell the people to do the next day?

- (13) tell the people to sanctify/purify themselves tomorrow

(40) What did the Lord say was necessary for them to fix their problem?

- (13) an evil thing is in the midst of us and we cannot defend ourselves against our enemies until we get rid of the cursed things among us

(41) What time of day did all the tribes come forward and present themselves?

- (14) In the morning

(42) What was the plan to identify the one(s) guilty?

- (14) In the morning all tribes must come forward and present themselves and the Lord will identify the guilty tribe. Then the families of this tribe, then the households, then eventually the specific man to blame will be identified and pointed out by God

(43) What was to be the punishment of the guilty person(s)?

- (15) The person who stole the cursed thing shall be burned with fire, he and all he has (owns) because he broke God's laws (covenant of the Lord) and brought tragedy on Israel

(44) Was this punishment too severe? Explain

- Optional – their honest answer to this question lends its way for great discussions

(45) Should the guilty person(s) have had a trial? Explain

- Optional – their honest answer to this question lends its way for great discussions

(46) If we handled these things this way today, do you think we would have the many prolonged problems we have?

- Optional – their honest answer to this question lends its way for great discussions
- No

(47) What time of day did Joshua comply?

- (16) Early in the morning

(48) What tribe, family and individual was singled out and identified as the culprit?

- (16) tribe of Judah, (17) family of Zarhites/Zerah & (18) Zimri/Zabdi, (18) individual – Achan

(49) What did Joshua ask the one identified to do?

- (19) give glory to the Lord God of Israel and confess now what you did

(50) What did he mean by this?

- To deny what you did is to say that God is a liar or that we are not hearing from God. Make it easier for yourself, please and confess it all hold nothing back to me, God already knows you will have to answer/repent to Him

(51) What did Joshua tell the one identified not to do?

- (19) don't lie/don't hide it from me

(52) What did Achan admit to?

- (20) "I have sinned against the Lord God of Israel"
- (20) he admitted what he did

(53) Should he have admitted all he did? Why not find out what Joshua knew first?

- Optional – their honest answer to this question lends its way for great discussions
- Yes
- Because he was given an opportunity to come clean and repent. It was not the time to play games. Either he should fully repent or he would still be in sin

(54) Why not assert his right to be silent?

- Optional – their honest answer to this question lends its way for great discussions
- He was trying to repent, which cannot be done in silence. One cannot repent or be forgiven for what they refuse to acknowledge

(55) What rights did Achan have that he surrendered?

- Optional – their honest answer to this question lends its way for great discussions
- He could have tried to deny it, not answered or demanded a trial

(56) Should he have gotten legal counsel first?

- Optional – their honest answer to this question lends its way for great discussions

(57) Should Achan have been afforded time to think before responding?

- Optional – their honest answer to this question lends its way for great discussions

(58) How is this old method different than today?

- Optional – their honest answer to this question lends its way for great discussions
- Today we rely on a man-made system, rather than go to God

(59) Should we go back to the old method? Explain

- Optional – their honest answer to this question lends its way for great discussions
- Yes, but we would have to be a society that had a relationship with God in order to do this. Leaders must also be submitted to God

(60) In your opinion, is the new method better? Why or why not?

- Optional – their honest answer to this question lends its way for great discussions

(61) List the differences and pros and cons of justice then and now.

- Optional – their honest answer to this question lends its way for great discussions
- Then when a ruler made a law or ruling it was carried out and there was no fighting it. Today we have an appeal system and cases that are fought years before a ruling is rendered.
- Even if the ruler realized he made a mistake and wanted to take his decree or promise back, he was unable to. Today with much protest and community activism unjust laws can be omitted or amended with time.
- Rulers often reigned until they died or were killed. Most leadership positions are time-barred today.

(62) Which of the five senses caused Achan's initial temptation?

- (21) His sight – He admitted, "When I <u>saw</u>..."

(63) What commandment(s) did he admit to breaking immediately thereafter?

- (21) He coveted and stole – "I coveted/wanted them and took them."

(64) Describe what was among the spoil.

- (21) A goodly Babylonish garment (beautiful robe imported from Babylon), 200 shekels of silver (200 silver coins), a wedge of gold of 50 shekels' weight (a bar of gold weighing more than a pound).

(65) Where did Joshua's messengers recover the stolen property?

- (22) Achan's tent and the silver underneath.

(66) How did they know where to find it?

- (21) Achan admitted where he hid it

(67) Why did they not punish Achan immediately after he confessed?

- Optional – their honest answer to this question lends its way for great discussions
- I believe they were unsure if he was being fully truthful
- If they had killed him too quickly they would not have gotten him to tell them where he hid the property

(68) Why do you think they ran to confirm and retrieve the items first?

- Optional – their honest answer to this question lends its way for great discussions
- Perhaps they thought the sooner they dealt with Achan and recovered the stolen property the quicker they could get back in God's graces

(69) They brought the items from Achan's tent to Joshua, and all the children of Israel and laid them before the Lord. Do you think they withheld any of the loot for themselves? Why?

- Optional – their honest answer to this question lends its way for great discussions
- No

- Fear that God would expose them & there would be severe consequences

(70) If you were a messenger would you bring it all back or keep some? Why?

- Optional – their honest answer to this question lends its way for great discussions

(71) Why was it important to occur in front of all the children of Israel?

- Optional – their honest answer to this question lends its way for great discussions
- To make an impact and set an example

(72) What did Joshua and all Israel take and bring to the valley of Achor?

- (24) Achan the son of Zerah, and all the stolen property (the silver, garment, and the wedge of gold), Achan's sons, daughters, oxen, asses (donkey), sheep, tent and all that he had

(73) Is there a reason why Achan and everything that belonged to him or was associated with him was collected together?

- Optional – their honest answer to this question lends its way for great discussions
- Yes

(74) Why not preserve some of the things of value and use them? Explain

- Optional – their honest answer to this question lends its way for great discussions
- They were tainted and a part of the sin committed that God said NOT to touch

(75) As Joshua said, "Why did you bring this trouble on us? Now the Lord shall trouble you." What did they do to punish Achan and discourage this from happening again?

- (25) All of Israel stoned Achan and his family with stones and burned their bodies

(76) Was the punishment more impactful by everyone participating and it being a public display?

- Optional – their honest answer to this question lends its way for great discussions
- Yes.

(77) Did you know the family could also receive punishment for something one of their relatives did?

- Optional – their honest answer to this question lends its way for great discussions

(78) Do you know of other examples in The Bible of this process?

- Optional – their honest answer to this question lends its way for great discussions
- David's first son with his mistress, Bathsheba, got sick and died – 2 Samuel 12
- Pharaoh cursed his first born and all firstborn Egyptians by defying God – Exodus 12:12
- Ananias and Sapphira were struck down dead – Acts 5
- Haman's 10 sons were hanged because of him – Esther 9:14

(79) If this happened today, would you like to be responsible if your parents or siblings sinned?

- Optional – their honest answer to this question lends its way for great discussions

(80) Your parents are responsible for violations you commit against others, is this fair? Explain

- Optional – their honest answer to this question lends its way for great discussions

(81) Why should you listen to your parents when they instruct you to do things that the Lord God agrees you are to obey, and you locate scriptures that also agree?
- Optional – their honest answer to this question lends its way for great discussions
- It is your obligation to obey your parents in the Lord or suffer consequences
- It is a huge responsibility to be punished for what another person in your family does
- The consequences for violating God's laws are severe

(82) Do you see ways that diverting from seeking the Lord has made crime, sin, corruption, and rebellion worse? Explain
- Optional – their honest answer to this question lends its way for great discussions

(83) Long ago the people decided they no longer wanted God to be the only judge (1 Samuel 8), and demanded to have a king rule them. Has this decision helped or hurt us?
- Optional – their honest answer to this question lends its way for great discussions

(84) What was piled on Achan?
- (26) A great heap of stones

(85) What was the place named where this happened at?
- (26) The place where this occurred was name the Valley of Achor/Valley of Trouble

(86) Why do you think God was so angry?
- Optional – their honest answer to this question lends its way for great discussions

(87) Was God's anger needless?
- Optional – their honest answer to this question lends its way for great discussions

(88) Was God's anger just?

- Optional – their honest answer to this question lends its way for great discussions

(89) Was God's anger causing a problem?

- Optional – their honest answer to this question lends its way for great discussions

(90) Would a leader in the armed services be just as angry, if a soldier chose not to follow orders, and committed an isolated act against direct orders to profit, and it cost other soldiers' lives?

- Optional – their honest answer to this question lends its way for great discussions

(91) Do you think soldiers are aware of all the reasons they are ordered to act and fight?

- Optional – their honest answer to this question lends its way for great discussions
- No

(92) Is it a soldier's job to know all the reasons or to just follow orders?

- Optional – their honest answer to this question lends its way for great discussions
- Just follow orders

(93) As youth with your parents being responsible and forced to answer for your actions should you be entitled to know all the facts, rationale and reasons before you obey, or should you just obey? Explain

- Optional – their honest answer to this question lends its way for great discussions
- Just obey

(94) Are the things your parents tell you to do for your own good and to teach you responsibility? Explain

- Optional – their honest answer to this question lends its way for great discussions

(95) Should you ever question your parents' orders when they are in compliance with God's laws and the moral code adopted by society.
- Optional – their honest answer to this question lends its way for great discussions
- No

(96) If the orders agree with man's laws but disagrees with God's laws, which should prevail?
- God's laws override man's laws.
- Optional – their honest answer to this question lends its way for great discussions

NOTES

Jeroboam – 1 Kings 13 (1-34)

Questions & Answers

1. The first individual mentioned in this chapter was characterized by what three words?
- (1) man of God
2. Where was he said to come out of?
- (1) Judah
3. How?
- (1) by the word of the Lord
4. Where was he going?
- (1) unto Bethel
5. Where was Jeroboam and what was he doing?
- (1) stood by the altar to burn incense
6. A child was said to be born unto whose house?
- (2) the house of David
7. What was the child supposed to be named?
- (2) Josiah
8. What was said to be burnt upon him?
- (2) men's bones shall be burnt
9. What was given to say the Lord had spoken?
- (3) a sign

10. When was it given?
- (3) the same day
11. What proof would evidence the Lord had spoken?
- (3) the altar shall be rent & the ashes upon it poured out
12. Who heard the saying of the messenger?
- (4) Jeroboam
13. Who was the messenger who delivered the saying?
- (4) & (5) man of God
14. What did he put forth from the altar?
- (4) his hand
15. What did he say?
- (4) "Lay hold on him"
16. How does the NLT version of scripture describe Jeroboam's mood and actions?
- (4) NLT version says King Jeroboam was very angry with the man
17. What symptoms did Jeroboam exhibit of his mood?
- (4) he pointed and shouted, "Seize that man!"
18. What happened next?
- (4) his hand dried up so he could not pull it in again (to himself)
19. Did his prophesy come true?
- (5) Yes
20. Explain how the prophesy did or did not come true:
- (5) The altar was rent, the ashes poured out from the altar
21. Who asked the man of God to entreat the Lord?
- (6) the king
22. What did he want the man of God to ask for or do?
- (6) for the man of God to pray and ask the Lord his God, to restore his hand
23. Did the man of God comply?

- (6) Yes.
24. Explain how the man of God did or did not comply:
- (6) He besought the Lord and the king's hand was restored and returned to its prior condition.
25. What did the king say to the man of God?
- (7) "Come home with me, and refresh thyself, and I will give thee a reward."
26. Did the man of God accept?
- (8) initially, no
27. What did the man of God reply?
- (8) "If thou wilt give me half thine house, I will not go in with thee, neither will I eat bread nor drink water in this place."
28. What did the man of God say that inspired and charged his response?
- (9) the word of the Lord
29. What directive did he say he was given?
- (9) "Eat no bread, nor drink water, nor turn again by the same way that thou camest."
30. Who did he say gave him this charge?
- (9) the Lord / the word of the Lord
31. Did he obey?
- (10) Yes.
32. How did he obey or disobey?
- (10) he went another way, and returned not by the way that he came to Bethel
33. Word spread to who by his relatives of what happened?
- (11) an old prophet
34. Where was this person when his relatives told him?
- (11) in Bethel
35. What did his relatives tell him?
- (11) all the works that the man of God had done that day in Bethel & the words he had spoken to the king

36. How were these relatives related to him?
- (11) they were his sons
37. Where did the relatives see the man of God coming from?
- (12) Judah
38. What did the man ask his relatives?
- (12) Which way did he go?
39. What did the prophet direct his relatives to do next?
- (13) "Saddle me the donkey"
40. Did his relatives obey? Explain
- (13) Yes.
- (13) They saddled the donkey
41. What did the prophet do with the donkey?
- (13) he rode it
42. What did he chase after?
- (14) he went after the man of God
43. Did he find who or what he was looking for? Explain
- (14) yes
- (14) he found him sitting under an oak
44. What did he ask?
- (14) "Art thou the man of God that camest from Judah?"
45. What reply did he receive?
- (14) "I am"
46. What invitation did he give?
- (15) Come home with me and eat bread
47. What response did his invitation receive?
- (16) "I may not return with thee, nor go in with thee: neither will I eat bread nor drink water with thee in this place:"
48. What rationalize was given to accept or reject the invitation?
- (17) "For it was said to me by the word of the Lord, Thou shalt eat no bread nor drink water there, nor turn again to go by the way that thou camest."

49. Did he owe an explanation as to why he refused the invitation? Explain
- Optional – their honest answer to this question lends its way for great discussions
- No. He should have simply said no and kept going on his journey
50. Does who is making the inquiry matter as to whether or not you should answer? Explain
- Optional – their honest answer to this question lends its way for great discussions
- Yes.
- Your parents deserve an answer.
51. Should we simply obey what God and our parents tell us without qualifying our actions? Explain
- Optional – their honest answer to this question lends its way for great discussions
- Yes
52. Who, in history, was an early example of saying too much when encouraged to defy God's rules?
- Optional – their honest answer to this question lends its way for great discussions
- Adam & Eve
53. What other times have you told others "no" and felt the need to explain why? Give examples
- Optional – their honest answer to this question lends its way for great discussions
- Offered drugs – "No, I can't, I get drug tested" "The judge said if I tested dirty again I'd get locked up"
- Ditch – "No, my parents told me if I ever ditch they'll…" "No, my folks check my attendance records"
- Attend party – "No, I'm not allowed to because…"

- Date – "I can't. My parents say I can't date until I'm 16"
- Wear make-up – "I'm not old enough yet" "I'll get caught"
- Come over and spend the night – "My parents say I can't visit unless a responsible adult is in your home with us"
- Friend comes to my home – "Visitors are not allowed in the home without an adult being there" "I must have permission"
- Accepting rides – "My parents told me not to accept a ride without their knowledge and consent"
- Throw party – "My dad has guns, and no one is allowed in certain rooms where he keep his weapons"

54. What advice would you give someone who is uncertain whether to abide by their parent's rules?

- Optional – their honest answer to this question lends its way for great discussions
- Run and turn away from people who have logical responses as to why you should listen to them and not God or your parents
- The more you give another voice your time and attention, it will convince you to yield
- When your spirit is unsettled pay attention
- Do not listen to conflicting advice
- Hold true and stand firm on the standards of God and the guidance from your parents or guardian

55. What excuses have you heard people give as to why they defied a trusted authority's rules?

- Optional – their honest answer to this question lends its way for great discussions
- I did not think you meant for me not to listen to them
- I thought it would be okay because of who was telling me to defy the rules

- But this is my coach, teacher, best friend's parents, minister, leader, mentor, etc.
- The opposing advice seemed to make sense at the time
- I did not know what else to do and they were pressuring me
- I was under a lot of peer pressure and wanted to be cool

56. What connection was pointed out to try to garner the invited person's trust?

- (18) I am a prophet, like you

57. Who did the prophet say spoke to him?

- (18) an angel

58. By whose authority?

- (18) by the word of the Lord

59. What did the prophet claim he was told to tell the man of God?

- (18) "Bring him back with thee into thine house, that he may eat bread and drink water."

60. Had the prophet told the truth?

- (18) No. He lied.

61. Was the man of God swayed by the prophet? Explain

- (19) Yes.
- (19) He went back with the prophet. He ate bread in his house and drank water.

62. Who did the word of the Lord come upon at the prophet's home?

- (20) the prophet that brought the man of God back

63. Where were they when this happened?

- (20) seated at the table

64. Did the man of God deserve chastisement? Explain

- Optional – their honest answer to this question lends its way for great discussions
- Yes.

- He was disobedient and did not heed the Lord's instructions
- He chose to listen to another man rather than to obey a clear mandate the Lord gave him

65. Who did God have admonish the man of God?
- (21) the prophet

66. What was the man of God told were his initial mistakes?
- (21) you disobeyed the mouth of the Lord
- (21) and have not kept the commandment which the Lord thy God commanded thee

67. What else was the man of God told he did wrong?
- (22) you came back
- (22) ate bread and drank water where the Lord told you to eat no bread and drink no water

68. What was he denied?
- (22) his carcass would not be upon the sepulcher of his fathers

69. What did the prophet do after the man of God finished eating?
- (23) the prophet saddled the man of God's donkey for him

70. What misfortune did the man of God encounter once he left?
- (24) a lion met him and slew him

71. Who or what stood by the man of God's carcass?
- (24) the donkey and the lion

72. Did the old prophet ever find out what happened to the man of God? Explain
- (25) Yes. Men passed by and saw the carcass and went back and informed the old prophet.

73. When the old prophet heard the news he knew it was the man of God this had happened to. How could he be so confident?
- He knew disobedience to God would result in consequences

- (26) It is the man of God who was disobedient unto the word of the Lord
- (26) The Lord had pre-warned him

74. Who did the old prophet say delivered the man of God and to whom?

- (26) The Lord has delivered him unto the lion

75. According to the old prophet was the man of God's death random and unpredictable? Explain

- No
- (26) the lion had torn and slain him according to the word of the Lord that was spoken beforehand

76. What did the old prophet direct to be done next?

- (27) he told his sons to saddle his donkey and they did

77. Did the prophet find what he went looking for? Explain

- (28) Yes.
- (28) He located the man of God's carcass

78. What else did he notice with the carcass that was unusual?

- (28) the donkey and the lion were still standing by the carcass
- (28) the lion had not eaten the carcass nor attacked the donkey

79. What did the old prophet do next?

- (29) he took up the carcass of the man of God, laid it on the donkey and brought it back with him and mourned and buried him/it

80. Where was the carcass buried?

- (30) in the old prophet's grave

81. How did the old prophet react upon laying the man of God's carcass in his own grave?

- (30) he mourned over him

82. What term of endearment did he use for the man of God?

- (30) my brother

83. Would you have responded like the old prophet? Explain

- Optional – their honest answer to this question lends its way for great discussions

84. What did the old prophet tell his sons to do with his body when he died?

- (31) "bury me in the sepulchre wherein the man of God is buried; lay my bones beside his bones"

85. Why did he say he was making this request?

- (32) "For the message the Lord told him to proclaim against the altar in Bethel and against the pagan shrines in the towns of Samaria will surely come true." (NLT)

86. Did Jeroboam change his life and repent? Explain

- (33) No. Jeroboam returned not from his evil way

- (33) He again put the lowest of people in high places as priests

- (33) Whoever wanted a high position as a priest, he consecrated them and let them become one

87. What was the end result of Jeroboam?

- (34) His behavior was known as a great sin and resulted in the destruction of his kingdom and the death of all his family (destroyed from off the face of the earth)

❖ Read Proverbs 6 and list the scriptures that would have been good for Jeroboam to have been mindful of:

A false witness who pours out lies, a person who sows discord among brothers. **Proverbs 6:19 KJV**
My son, obey your father's commands, and don't neglect your mother's teaching. **Proverbs 6:20 KJV**
Keep their words always in your heart. Tie them around your neck. **Proverbs 6:21 KJV**

NOTES

Bartimaeus – Mark 10:46-52 & Luke 18:35-43

Questions & Answers

1. What revered person came to Jericho?
- (37) Jesus of Nazareth
2. What others were said to be with this person?
- (46) his disciples and a great number of people
3. Whose son sat by the highway?
- (46) Timaeus
4. What was his name?
- (46) Bartimaeus
5. What was he doing there?
- (46) & (35) begging
6. He was characterized as having what disability?
- (46) & (35) blind
7. What got his attention? What did he see?
- (47) He heard Jesus was passing by
- (36) He heard the multitude pass by
- He didn't see anything, he was blind. This was a trick question.
8. What did he ask people?
- (36) he asked what the noise he heard meant
9. What was he told?

90

- (37) that Jesus of Nazareth was passing by
10. Did he know this passerby personally?
- No
11. Why do you believe he called out to this passerby?
- Optional – their honest answer to this question lends its way for great discussions
- He heard Jesus was the messiah who healed and did miracles
- He recognized it may be his only chance to reach out to Jesus
- The messiah was right there nearby, a once in a lifetime opportunity for Bartimaeus
12. What did he call out to him saying?
- (47) & (38) Jesus, thou son of David, have mercy on me
13. Who reacted and what was the reaction?
- (48) the people who had been following Jesus charged/reprimanded Bartimaeus to be silent
- (39) the multitude passing by rebuked Bartimaeus and told him he should hold his peace/shut up
14. Why do you think others reacted to him this way?
- Optional – their honest answer to this question lends its way for great discussions
- They viewed Bartimaeus as an insignificant beggar who should not have the nerve to bother such an important man as Jesus
- Maybe they wanted to spare Jesus of this man begging him
- They thought they could decide who had the right to approach Jesus and who was not worthy
15. Did others' reaction and criticism affect this man?
- (48) No. He ignored them and cried out even more
- (39) No. He cried even more, "Thou son of David, have

mercy on me."
16. Why do you think he was able to dismiss them?
- Because he was tired of his condition
- He was the one living with the limitations and he was not about to let others make him miss out
- His desire to be healed far surpassed his need to be accepted by the people and follow them
- Their opinion was not the one that mattered to Bartimaeus. Only Jesus' opinion had value and since Jesus was not telling him to be quiet, Bartimaeus was determined to cry out to Jesus.
17. Have you let the comments and critiques of others cause you to lose out on a blessing from God? Explain
- Optional – their honest answer to this question lends its way for great discussions
18. What did the passerby do as a result?
- (49) He stood still. Bartimaeus' persistence got Jesus' attention
- (49) Jesus commanded that Bartimaeus be brought to Him
- (40) Jesus stood and had Bartimaeus brought to Him
19. What hypocritical thing did the critics do when the passerby was receptive to him?
- (49) The people who had chastised him for calling out to Jesus were the very same people who seconds later had a completely opposite response. Since Jesus had called for him they were now telling Bartimaeus to "Be of good comfort, rise; he calleth thee."
- One minute they are practically telling him Jesus did not want to be bothered with him so he needed to be quiet. The next minute they are telling him in essence to be happy because Jesus wanted him and was calling for him.
20. What should this tell you about people?

- Optional – their honest answer to this question lends its way for great discussions
- People are fickle and unreliable
- Do not put your faith in people or rely on them to encourage and motivate you
- Others will confuse you with their instability and fluctuation
- You need to go after what you want and stand firm on your convictions and not on the criticisms of others

21. What did the passerby ask him?
- (51) "What wilt thou that I should do unto thee?"
22. State his answer to the question:
- (51) "Lord, that I might receive my sight"
- (41) "Lord, that I may receive my sight"
23. How did Jesus respond?
- He gave him something to do that required an act of faith
24. What did Jesus tell him to do?
- (52) "Go thy way"
- (42) "Receive thy sight"
25. What did Jesus say made him whole and saved this man?
- (52) & (42) his faith
26. How long did it take before the man saw any results? What were the results if any?
- (52) & (43) immediately – he received his sight
27. Who got credit in the end? Explain
- (52) Jesus – Bartimaeus followed Him
- (43) Jesus & God – Bartimaeus followed Jesus, glorifying God
- (43) God – all the people who saw Bartimaeus get healed gave praise unto God
28. How did the two books of The Bible differ in how they ended this story?

- (52) Mark ends with Bartimaeus immediately upon receiving his sight, following Jesus. Even a blind man could see who was responsible for him being healed.
- (43) Luke ends with immediately upon Bartimaeus receiving his sight, that not only did Bartimaeus follow Christ and glorify God, but all the people who saw it gave praise unto God as well.

NOTES

Born Blind – John 9

Questions & Answers

1. Jesus was passing by and noticed a man with what type of condition?
- (1) blindness
2. How long had he been in that condition?
- (1) since birth
3. What did Jesus' disciples attribute to the cause of this man's condition?
- (2) sin
4. What question did his disciples ask him regarding who was responsible for the man's condition?
- (2) "Who did sin, this man, or his parents, that he was born blind?"
5. How did Jesus respond?
- (3) Jesus answered, "Neither hath this man sinned, nor his parents: but that the works of God should be made manifest in him."
- (4) I must work the works of him that sent me, while it is day: the night cometh, when no man can work.
- (5) As long as I am in the world, I am the light of the world.
6. Interpret what you believe Jesus meant by this response:

- Optional – their honest answer to this question lends its way for great discussions
- (3) The condition was not a punishment God handed down because of a sin this man or his parents committed. The man's blindness was simply a condition that was necessary for God to show people that He is a healer. It does not matter how long the condition existed, nothing is impossible for him. The fact that this man was known in his community helped lend credibility and increased the faith of others in God
- (4) Jesus had to show forth God's power while on the earth. This was the time while people were being illuminated with knowledge and had their eyes, ears and hearts open. There would come a time when the enemy would blind the eyes of people and they would not be open to a movement of God and He would be unable to demonstrate His power because of doubt and unbelief.
- (5) As long as Christ was on earth, He would be able to expose the truth, enlighten the world and lead others to the path to God
7. What did Jesus make and how did he make it?
- (6) spittle
- (6) he spat on the ground and made clay
8. What did he do next?
- (7) he anointed the eyes of the blind man with the clay
9. If you heard this going on by you would you have remained and let this happen to you if you were this man? Explain
- Optional – their honest answer to this question lends its way for great discussions
- Hearing the hacking sound of someone spitting before me would have probably had me leaving. To have a stranger putting mud on my eyes would not have been received well

by me. I would only see myself sticking around if I knew it was Jesus doing this and knowing there was a potential of being made better

10. Jesus instructed this man to do what?
- (7) "Go, wash in the pool of Siloam."
11. What word is interpreted and what is the interpretation?
- (7) pool of Siloam – Sent
12. Did the man do what Jesus instructed him to?
- (7) yes
13. What resulted?
- (7) he returned seeing
14. People who knew him when they saw him, what did they wonder about?
- (8) Whether the man they saw before them was indeed the same man they knew to be blind who sat and begged
15. Who were these people?
- (8) Neighbors and members of the community
16. What were people heard saying?
- (9) That is him
- (9) That is someone who looks like him
17. Did the man have anything to say? Explain
- (9) Yes. He confirmed he was indeed the man in question
18. The people wanted to know what about this man?
- (10) how his eyes were opened
19. How did he answer?
- (11) A man, Jesus made clay, and anointed my eyes. He told me to go to the pool of Siloam, and wash. I went and washed and received my sight.
20. Then what did they want to know?
- (12) where Jesus was
21. What did the man answer?
- (12) he did not know where Jesus was

22. What did the people do next?
- (13) they brought him to the Pharisees
23. Was there any significance to when Jesus healed this man?
- (14) Yes – it was done on the Sabbath day
24. Why was this a problem?
- Optional – their honest answer to this question lends its way for great discussions
- No man was allowed to work on the Sabbath, to do so was punishable by law
- It gave the religious leaders an opening to criticize and attempt to paint Christ as a lawbreaker
- The critics took this as an opportunity to show Jesus was in direct violation of the written law
25. What did the Pharisees want to know of this man?
- (15) how he had received his sight
26. What did the man answer?
- (15) clay was put on his eyes, he washed it off and began to see
27. What did the Pharisees surmise from the information the man gave them?
- (16) Jesus is not of God
28. Why did they draw this conclusion?
- (16) because Jesus had healed on the Sabbath
29. What did others think of Jesus?
- (16) Others said, "How can a man that is a sinner do such miracles?"
30. Were the Pharisees and others' opinions aligned about Jesus? Explain
- (16) No
- (16) there was division among them
31. Today, does everyone agree about who Jesus is? Explain

- Optional – their honest answer to this question lends its way for great discussions
- No. So don't go by the confusion and issues of others, make your own decision with open eyes
32. They asked the man who was healed his opinion of what Jesus did to him, what did he say?
- (17) He is a prophet
33. Was the man who was healed asked this only once?
- (17) no, he was asked more than once
34. Explain why you think that was?
- I think they were trying to get him to badmouth Jesus and to change his opinion
- They probably pointed out how could you be okay with a man who spit in the dirt and put mud in your eyes?
- They were attempting to get him to doubt his healing so the people would stop following Christ
35. Is there a danger in trying to prove how the Lord works? Should it matter?
- Optional – their honest answer to this question lends its way for great discussions
- Yes & No. Yes, because the Lord operates off of faith and does not conform to man's logic. Trying to apply worldly rules to a faith God who defies worldly constraints of proof can be dangerous. No, because the word of God is true and I do not believe how the Lord works can be disproved.
- In my opinion, it does not matter. When it comes to my faith, only my opinion and the Lord's opinion matters. It is not worth my time trying to convince others what I believe and proving my experience with God. Whether they accept the truth or not has no significance on the truth so in that respect it should not matter.
36. What is your best evidence of the Lord working in your life?

- Optional – their honest answer to this question lends its way for great discussions
- Being a living example, speaking, and showing behavior that lines up with what Jesus preached
- Living by His standards and biblical principles
37. What was the next attempt that was made to derail the healing?
- (18) the Jews made it known they did not believe the man had been blind and received his sight
38. Who did the Jews summon that changed their opinion?
- (18) the blind man's parents
39. What 3 questions did they ask these experts?
- (19) 1 – Is this your son?
- (19) 2 – Did you say he was born blind?
- (19) 3 – If that is the case how is it possible that he can now see?
40. How did they answer the 3 questions?
- (20) 1 – Yes, we know this is our son
- (20) 2 – Yes, he was born blind
- (21) 3 – How he is able to see, we do not know
41. What other question were they also obviously asked based on their added reply? List the possible question along with their answer:
- (21) Who healed him? – We do not know who opened his eyes
42. What did they say to remove the spotlight from on them?
- (21) He is an adult. Ask him. He can speak for himself.
43. Who and what were these experts afraid of?
- (22) the Jews
- (22) the Jews had let it be known that if anyone confessed Jesus as Christ, he would be expelled from the synagogue

44. Do you think their involvement with the synagogue was important to them? Explain
- Optional – their honest answer to this question lends its way for great discussions
- Yes
- (23) They were quick and careful to get the Jews off their back and direct the Jews to ask their son directly. They did not want to be put out of the synagogue affirming Jesus who they did not know
- To throw their son under the bus and not come to his defense means they found their connection to the synagogue more important to them
45. Who did they call next to question?
- (24) the man who was healed of blindness
46. What did they say to this person?
- (24) give God praise
- (24) we know that this man (Jesus) is a sinner
47. Was there anything wrong with what they said to this person?
- Optional – their honest answer to this question lends its way for great discussions
- Give God praise – good advice but Jesus is God/Lord and was due praise as well
- We know this man is a sinner – they were attempting to discount Jesus without any evidence, this is wrong
48. Did this person argue with the advice he was given? Explain
- (25) no, he simply stated facts
- (25) he refused to engage in a debate of whether Jesus was a sinner or not, and stated he did not know
49. What fact did he point out that the Jews could not refute?
- (25) I know that I was blind and now I see
50. What did they question him about next?

- (26) What did Jesus do to you?
- (26) How did he open your eyes?

51. Would these questions have gotten you angry? Explain

- Optional – their honest answer to this question lends its way for great discussions
- Yes – they were being patronizing
- It was annoying and their persistence would not have made me happy.

52. How did the man respond?

- (27) He refused to answer because he had already told them and answered these questions

53. Did this man feel heard? Explain

- (27) no
- (27) he basically told them if you have chosen not to hear my answer before, what guarantee is there that you would hear my answer now?

54. What question(s) did the man ask them as a reply?

- (27) Why do you want to know? Are you planning on trying to be one of his disciples?

55. How did the Jews respond to him?

- (28) they reviled / cursed him
- (28) they called him names and tried to imply that he was following a ministry and system of belief that was different and against what Moses taught

56. What anger patterns and styles did the Jews demonstrate?

- Mind Reading – they were certain to claim they knew how this man thought and believed and their solid arrogance in their own assessment got them angry with the man
- Magnification – they took a positive event and made it into a big deal and major interrogation session
- Escalation – they used the letter of the law of the Sabbath

day and twisted the intent

- Imperative Thinking – their rule was that a common beggar had no right to challenge them as religious leaders and should have been silent. No man like Jesus who had not paid his dues and been endorsed by the church was worthy of creating a following that gained more respect and influence than theirs.
- Repetitive Anger – they were still jealous and angry at Jesus because the people believed in Him, followed Him and hung on His every word. Yet they continued to try to put Him down and discredit those who were convinced He was Christ. They were unwilling to address their jealousy, fears and ignorance in a positive way, and tried to be sneaky behind the scenes.

57. Did the Jews give a mature or immature reply? Explain
- Immature
- It was childish of them to decide since they had no intelligent response they cursed him and had him thrown out. Rather than having an intelligent or mature discussion, they felt the blind man, a commoner had outwit them and they used their position of power to retaliate.

58. Who did they compare Jesus to?
- (29) Moses

59. Did Jesus measure up to this other person in their opinion? Explain
- (29) No. They said they knew of Moses, but Jesus they did not know. They said they knew God spoke to Moses, but they did not even know where Jesus was from

60. In your own words, what did the man have to say about what happened to him and how they were responding to it?
- (30) He questioned why they were trying to put down a situation that should be celebrated because it was a

marvelous thing that happened.

- (30) He found it hard to believe their questions were about where Jesus was so they could challenge or arrest Him, rather than caring about what a miraculous thing that occurred that they were privy to
- (30) "Jesus opened my eyes, why aren't we applauding that and hailing Him for that?"

61. This man was not an expert in religious doctrine yet what did he say that demonstrated wisdom?

- (31) we know that God does not hear sinners
- (31) if any man is a worshipper of God, does His will, God hears him
- (32) since the beginning of time no man has ever been known to heal blinded eyes, or the eyes of one born blind
- (33) if Jesus were not of God He would not have been able to heal him like He did

62. Did it appear the Jews were receptive to the man's logic and wisdom? Explain

- (34) No, they were insulted
- (34) They basically told him, "You were blind because you were born in sin. Who are you to think that you can attempt to teach us?"
- (34) they cast him out

63. What vanity was in full operation in the Jews and the Pharisees?

- Optional – their honest answer to this question lends its way for great discussions
- Pride

64. Who was told the man had been cast out and searched for him until he found him?

- (35) Jesus

65. What did Jesus ask him?

- (35) Do you believe on the Son of God?

66. Was the man angry about being asked this question? Explain

- No, he was humble

67. If the Jews had asked this man the exact same question do you think he would have responded the same way?

- Optional – their honest answer to this question lends its way for great discussions

- No, because the Jews had malicious intent and Jesus had good intent

68. Explain what may have been different to solicit a different reaction.

- His interpretation

- The Jews were trying to discredit him and his experience, so he had good reason to be suspicious of their questions and statements. Jesus however had gained this man's trust

69. What did the man's response to Jesus show about his stance?

- (36) Who is he, Lord – he acknowledged that Jesus was Lord

- (36) that I might believe – he was eager to know, learn and believe

70. How did Jesus answer?

- (37) you have seen Him and are talking to Him right now

71. How much convincing did it take for the man to believe? Explain

- (38) very little, just Jesus' word

- (38) he said, "Lord, I believe" and worshipped Him

72. What was Jesus' reply?

- (39) I came into this world to judge it, so those who cannot see may see; and so those who see may be made blind

73. What do you think this statement means?

- Optional – their honest answer to this question lends its way for great discussions
- By coming to the world He would be the ultimate expert and authority on what was true and just
- His judgment and adjudication was sure to turn experts into ignorant amateurs, amateurs into experts, the wise into the foolish, the foolish into the wise, the seeing into the blind and the blind into the seeing

74. Did the Pharisees appear to understand what Jesus meant by his statement? Explain

- Optional – their honest answer to this question lends its way for great discussions
- (40) they may not have fully understood, but they knew that He was referencing them as being blind
- I believe they recognized He was calling them out for thinking themselves more highly than they should

75. What did Jesus say in response?

- (41) If you were blind, you would have no sin. You claim to see so you are acknowledging your guilt

NOTES

SUGGESTIONS

*So shall my word be that goeth forth out of my mouth: it shall
not return unto me void, but it shall accomplish that which I
please, and it shall prosper in the thing whereto I sent it.*
Isaiah 55:11 KJV

I invite you to continue studying the scriptures with me. Although
there are many options you have available to continue your
search for answers, I highly recommend The Bible as the
ultimate source of truth. Below are some suggested sections
and websites that you may find helpful in your journey:

1. The 10 Commandments
- Memorize and get to know these commandments well
- *Exodus 20:1-17*

2. Proverbs
- There are a total of 31 chapters. Read a chapter each day
  for at least a year. Select at least one verse to meditate on
  for the whole day
- *Proverbs 1-31*

3. Psalms
- Review the worship of the person (David) who God referred to as, "a man after my own heart"
- *Psalms 1-150*

4. Apostle Paul
- Don't just read about him, study the life of the apostle Paul
- Find out about his radical conversion and how he was persecuted by the religious community
- *Acts, Romans, 1 Corinthians, 2 Corinthians, Galatians, Ephesians, Philippians, Colossians, 1 Thessalonians, 2 Thessalonians, 1 Timothy, 2 Timothy, Titus, Philemon, Hebrews*

5. The Beatitudes
- This section is considered a sermon by Jesus on how to be blessed and happy
- *Matthew 5:3-12*

6. Internet Resources
- http://www.BlueletterBible.org
  - You can read any scripture and specify the translation
- http://www.Google.com
  - Search any topic you want scripture references on.
- http://www.meetup.com
  - Find and/or set-up a study group in your area
- http://www.lightsource.com
  - Access sermons from prolific influential pastors

7. The 2 Greatest Commandments
- Jesus summed up the just of the scriptures into two

commandments, they are vital to living a righteous life
* *Matthew 22:35-40 and Mark 12:28-34*

The important thing is that you delve into the word, how you choose to do this is not as significant.

If you would like to access some of my additional resources and have not already done so, please sign up and enroll in these two introductory online courses:

Anger Management
https://rental-match-academy.thinkific.com/courses/anger-management2

4 Personality Types
https://rental-match-academy.thinkific.com/courses/4-personality-types

Avoid simply going through The Bible and *grow* through it!

HELPFUL SCRIPTURES

*These were more noble than those in Thessalonica, in that
they received the word with all readiness of mind, and
searched the scriptures daily, whether those things were so.*
Acts 17:11 KJV

<u>Why we should study The Bible</u>:
(15) The simple believeth every word: but the prudent man
looketh well to his going. (16) A wise man feareth, and departeth
from evil: but the fool rageth, and is confident.
Proverbs 14:15-16 KJV
(8) The wise in heart will receive commandments: but a prating
fool shall fall. (9) He that walketh uprightly walketh surely: but he
that perverteth his ways shall be known.
(17) He is in the way of life that keepeth instruction: but he that
refuseth reproof erreth. **Proverbs 10:8-9, 17 KJV**

<u>Accept correction & when you know better, do better</u>
(6) A scorner seeketh wisdom, and findeth it not: but knowledge
is easy unto him that understandeth. (7) Go from the presence
of a foolish man, when thou perceives not in him the lips of
knowledge. (8) The wisdom of the prudent is to understand his

way: but the folly of fools is deceit.
Proverbs 14:6-8 KJV
(9) Fools make fun of guilt, but the godly acknowledge it and seek reconciliation. **Proverbs 14:9 NLT**

What proactive action can you take right now?

(11) And that, knowing the time, that now it is high time to awake out of sleep: for now is our salvation nearer than when we believed. (12) The night is far spent, the day is at hand: let us therefore cast off the works of darkness, and let us put on the armour of light. (13) Let us walk honestly, as in the day; not in rioting and drunkenness, not in chambering and wantonness, not in strife and envying. (14) But put ye on the Lord Jesus Christ, and make not provision for the flesh, to fulfil the lusts thereof. **Romans 13:11-14 KJV**
(9) Those things, which ye have both learned, and received, and heard, and seen in me, do: and the God of peace shall be with you. **Philippians 4:9 KJV**

Wisdom can be found in God's word:

(8) All the words of my mouth are in righteousness; there is nothing froward or perverse in them. (9) They are all plain to him that understandeth, and right to them that find knowledge.
(32) Now therefore hearken unto me, O ye children: for blessed are they that keep my ways. (33) Hear instruction, and be wise, and refuse it not. **Proverbs 8:8-9, 32-33**
(31) The ear that heareth the reproof of life abideth among the wise. (32) He that refuseth instruction despiseth his own soul: but he that heareth reproof getteth understanding. (33) The fear of the Lord is the instruction of wisdom; and before honour is humility. **Proverbs 15:31-33 KJV**

<u>Have hope in the future and not in what you can see now:</u>
(16) That is why we never give up. Though our bodies are dying, our spirits are being renewed every day. (17) For our present troubles are quite small and won't last very long. Yet they produce for us an immeasurably great glory that will last forever! (18) So we don't look at the troubles we can see right now; rather, we look forward to what we have not yet seen. For the troubles we see will soon be over, but the joys to come will last forever. **2 Corinthians 4:16-18 NLT**
So we have stopped evaluating others by what the world thinks about them. Once I mistakenly thought of Christ that way, as though he were merely a human being, How differently I think about him now! **2 Corinthians 5:16 NLT**

LETTER FROM THE AUTHOR

Growing up is a challenging experience. Every child needs a safe place to go and someone they can talk to. It would be nice if that safe haven was their home and the people they could trust to share their problems with were their parents. This would be ideal.

Unfortunately, for a variety of reasons, necessary conversations are not taking place. There are many teens with built up frustrations and nowhere they know of to release it. It behooves us as adults to initiate discussions with the young people in our lives we care about and see every day.

If you have no children of your own, yet have a passion for working with youth, there are things that you can do. I implore you, please locate a group in your community where you can volunteer your time, and help guide the youth of today who struggle with issues and feel they have no one to talk to. Contact your local churches, schools, community centers and youth programs. Find a way to help parents guide their children down the right path.

Sometimes an empathetic ear can make a big difference in a young person's life. Please find a way to plug in somewhere and become a positive mentor. They have been told so many lies, is it not time someone taught them how to find the truth? I pray that my exercises will inspire professing Christians to step up and be salt and light to a confused and lost generation. Whatever you do, just do something constructive!

PRAYER OF SALVATION

How do you get saved? What is the prayer of salvation? What words do you say?

I do not pretend to speak for God. Many will say you must be in a church, or accept Christ publicly in front of others for it to count. Some say you must be baptized a specific way. I say, what does The Bible say about how to attain salvation?

For God so loved the world, that he gave his only begotten Son, that whosoever believeth in him should not perish, but have everlasting life.   **John 3:16 KJV**

(9) That if thou shalt confess with thy mouth the Lord Jesus, and shalt believe in thine heart that God hath raised him from the dead, thou shalt be saved. (10) For with the heart man believeth unto righteousness; and with the mouth confession is made unto salvation.

Romans 10:9-10 KJV

(9) I am the door: by me if any man enter in, he shall be saved, and shall go in and out, and find pasture. (10) The thief cometh not, but for to steal and to kill, and to destroy: I am come that they might have life, and that they might have it more abundantly. **John 10:9-10 KJV**

Jesus saith unto him, I am the way, the truth, and the life: no man cometh unto the Father, but by me.

John 14:6 KJV

(10) Be it known unto you all, and to all the people of Israel, that by the name of Jesus Christ of Nazareth, whom ye crucified, whom God raised from the dead, even by him doth this man stand here before you whole. (11) This is the stone which was set at nought of you builders, which is become the head of the corner. (12) Neither is there salvation in any other: for there is none other name under heaven given among men, whereby we must be saved.

Acts 4:10-12 KJV

Based on these scriptures the qualifiers are:
- I must know and acknowledge **JESUS** is the only way to God
- I must BELIEVE in Christ Jesus (Son of God)
- I must CONFESS Jesus with my mouth and BELIEVE in my heart God raised him from the dead

www.ingramcontent.com/pod-product-compliance
Lightning Source LLC
Chambersburg PA
CBHW021326060726
47591CB00006B/1889